Write Your Own

Mystery Stories

Tish Farrell

Your writing quest

Do you always figure out 'whodunnit' and think you could solve perplexing mysteries of your own? This book will give you all the clues and insider tips you need to craft an intriguing story to keep your readers guessing.

Your first case, as a trainee writer, is to track down your untold story and turn it into a gripping tale that hooks your readers from the first line. You must do some serious detective work too; stake-outs and investigations to look for mysterious possibilities.

To help you on your search, there will be a variety of training and brainstorming exercises that will develop your creative writing skills. There will also be plenty of examples from famous mystery writers' works to inspire you. So now you can get case-cracking.

Good luck!

Copyright © ticktock Entertainment Ltd 2006
First published in Great Britain in 2006 by ticktock Media Ltd.,
Unit 2, Orchard Business Centre, North Farm Road, Tunbridge Wells, Kent, TN2 3XF
We would like to thank: Egan-Reid Ltd for their help with this book.
ISBN 1 86007 922 9 PB
Printed in China
3 4 5 6 7 8 9 10
A CIP catalogue record for this book is available from the British Library.

CONTENTS

WANT TO BE A WRITER?

This book aims to give you the tools to write your own mystery fiction. Learn how to craft believable characters, perfect plots, and satisfying beginnings, middles and endings.

Step-by-step instruction

The pages throughout the book include numbers providing step-by-step instructions or a series of options that will help you to master certain parts of the writing process. To create beginnings, middles and ends, for example, complete 19 simple steps.

Chronological progress

You can follow your progress by using the bar located on the bottom of each page. The orange colour tells you how far along the story-writing process you have got. As the blocks are filled out, so your story will be gathering pace...

---

36 GOOD BEGINNINGS

❼ Create an intriguing beginning

Mystery stories should begin with a mystery. An intriguing first sentence is a good start. Readers must know at once that there will be unusual riddles to solve. But a mystery story is also about people and the heroes will have their own problems, or at least some very pressing reason to solve the mystery.

❽ Hook your reader

At the start of your story, you bait your hook with the tastiest titbits, so the reader bites. But you also must lay solid foundations, so that as you build your story, you end up with something strong. It is therefore essential that you know your mystery story's ending before you start writing. Then you can work backwards, dropping hints and clues in advance. This is called foreshadowing and it is an important storytelling tool.

Case study

Wilkie Collins (below) said this about how to treat readers: Make 'em laugh, make 'em cry, make 'em wait.

Now it's your turn

Good beginnings

Write the opening scene of your story. Introduce the hero and the mystery. If possible, include some action. Look at ways to hook readers' interest and curiosity. Or be spooky. Also decide if there's any important information that needs to be slipped in at this point. When you have finished, go back and concentrate on your first sentence. Is it as exciting as you can make it?

| GETTING STARTED | WRITING STYLES AND IDEAS | CREATING CHARACTERS | VIEWPOINTS |

Each section explains a key part of the writing process, from creating believable landscapes and characters to structuring a story itself. Once you have got to the end of the bar, your story is ready! *Write Your Own...* ends with looking at the next step – what do you want to do next? Write a sequel? Tell a story from the viewpoint of another character in the first story? Or perhaps try something completely different...

Box features

Appearing throughout the book, these four different colour-coded box types help you with the writing process by providing inspiration, examples from other books, background details and hints and tips.

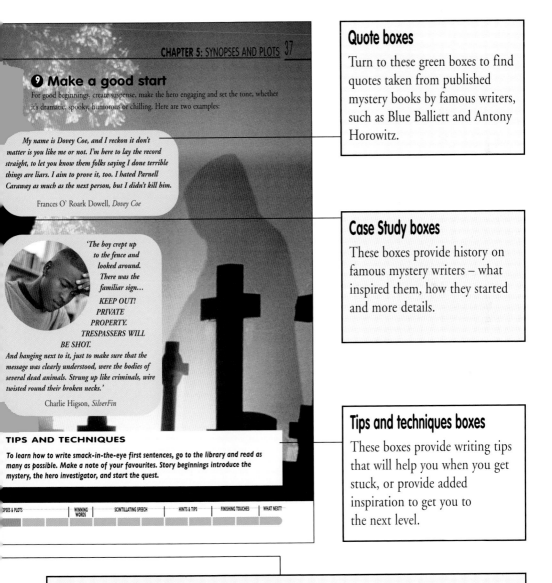

CHAPTER 5: SYNOPSES AND PLOTS 37

❾ Make a good start

For good beginnings, create suspense, make the hero engaging and set the tone, whether it's dramatic, spooky, humorous or chilling. Here are two examples:

My name is Dovey Coe, and I reckon it don't matter is you like me or not. I'm here to lay the record straight, to let you know them folks saying I done terrible things are liars. I aim to prove it, too. I hated Parnell Caraway as much as the next person, but I didn't kill him.

Frances O' Roark Dowell, *Dovey Coe*

'The boy crept up to the fence and looked around. There was the familiar sign...
KEEP OUT!
PRIVATE
PROPERTY.
TRESPASSERS WILL
BE SHOT.
And hanging next to it, just to make sure that the message was clearly understood, were the bodies of several dead animals. Strung up like criminals, wire twisted round their broken necks.'

Charlie Higson, *SilverFin*

TIPS AND TECHNIQUES

To learn how to write smack-in-the-eye first sentences, go to the library and read as many as possible. Make a note of your favourites. Story beginnings introduce the mystery, the hero investigator, and start the quest.

OPSES & PLOTS | WINNING WORDS | SCINTILLATING SPEECH | HINTS & TIPS | FINISHING TOUCHES | WHAT NEXT!

Quote boxes

Turn to these green boxes to find quotes taken from published mystery books by famous writers, such as Blue Balliett and Antony Horowitz.

Case Study boxes

These boxes provide history on famous mystery writers – what inspired them, how they started and more details.

Tips and techniques boxes

These boxes provide writing tips that will help you when you get stuck, or provide added inspiration to get you to the next level.

Now it's your turn boxes

These boxes provide a chance for you to put into practice what you have just been reading about. Simple, useful and fun exercises to help you build your writing skills.

WHY DO WRITERS WRITE?

You can learn a great deal from hearing how published writers became successful. All will say that it took them a long time, and that they wrote rubbish at first. If you asked them, they would doubtless add that they never stop learning their craft.

Blue Balliett

Her first novel, the art mystery *Chasing Vermeer*, is published now in 11 languages. She started writing it 1999 when she was teaching at a Chicago school where the story is set. Her students were writing art mysteries so she thought she would write one too. She rewrote her story five times before she was happy with it.

Anthony Horowitz

The inventor of the reluctant schoolboy spy, Alex Rider, Antony Horowitz, knew he wanted to write from the age of eight when he asked for a typewriter for his birthday. It was about this time he was sent away to boarding school where he had a miserable time and is still getting over it today. He was an overweight, unhappy son of a millionaire father, and he draws on many of his childhood experiences in his writing. He says he's lucky to have two assistant editors at home – his two teenage sons!

Joan Lowery Nixon

She wrote more than 140 books during her prestigious award-winning career. She was first published at ten years old – a poem called *Springtime*. Other works include *The Kidnapping of Christina Lattimore* and *A Place to Belong (The Orphan Train Adventures)*. She says that for her, a mystery always began with a question: what would it be like to live in a house where a murder had taken place; or how would she feel if a best friend had been arrested for murder. Here are a few of her tips:

Creating suspense in a mystery story is not just a matter of keeping readers guessing. Suspense calls for the emotional responses of anxiety, excitement, and fear…Make a list of clues that you can use in your story. One should be the crucial clue…one piece of important information that helps the main character finally solve the mystery.

Vicki Berger Erwin

She is author of the *Elizabeth Bryan Mystery* series (*The Disappearing Card Trick* etc) and has also written for *The Baby-Sitters Club*. Before she starts writing, she says she has to know:

- The end of her mystery;
- Why the detective wants to find the solution;
- The villain's motive.

Then she tries to make the mystery personal. The 'detective' wants to solve the case because it affects a friend or family member or something else they really care for.

Meg Cabot's writing day

(author of *The Mediator Series* and *The Princess Diaries*)

- Breakfast at 9am. Reads the paper until 10am
- Writes in bed, in her pyjamas until 6 or 7pm – unless she has a lunch date!
- She always writes on her laptop because her handwriting is so bad.

She says: *If you want to be a writer, you have to read! It doesn't matter what you read, just read as much as possible.*

FIRST THINGS FIRST

Unlike private eyes and real police detectives, mystery writers solve their 'whodunnits' with pen and paper or on a computer in their own homes. They may visit the library or use the Internet to check facts or research an idea, but otherwise they can work in comfort and quiet.

❶ Gather your writing materials

As you follow the advice in this book, some of the following will help you organize your plotting and planning:

- A small notebook that you carry everywhere
- Pens with different coloured ink
- Coloured post-it notes for research ideas and marking places in books
- Stick-on stars for

highlighting your writing notes

- Folders for storing up good story ideas
- Spiral-bound notebook and scrap paper
- Dictionary, thesaurus and encyclopaedia
- A computer or word processor (although this is not essential).

❷ Find a writing place

Before you start, you need an incident room or special writing place. This will probably be your bedroom, but being a sleuth, you may like to write where you can watch people – in the park, at school, in your local café. Have fun discovering where your very best writing place might be, but remember, wherever it is, to sit up straight while you work. Hunched up writing blocks the flow of oxygen to the brain, and might make you lose the plot.

❸ Create a writing zone

You may also need some extra creativity triggers. These could be:

• Music that makes you think clearly

• A magnifying glass to look at things in minute detail

• Binoculars for neighbourhood-sleuthing

• A hat that you only wear when you're writing (Sherlock Holmes had his deerstalker.

You could make or customize a hat you already have).

• Puzzles, games and books on code-cracking – anything to exercise your powers of deduction.

Spend time choosing these things. Your writing place is special to you. Special things are going to happen there.

TIPS AND TECHNIQUES

Once you have found your writing place, the golden rule of becoming a real writer is: Go there as often as possible. And write something!

❹ Develop detective skills

Writers and investigators have a lot in common: sharp eyes for detail, hunches about things that don't fit and incurable curiosity. But mystery writers must think up crimes that challenge both their sleuth and readers. They must create a believable, exciting story that readers can't put down.

❺ Put in the groundwork

Learning to become a writer can take a long time. You must train yourself to write regularly, not just when you feel inspired. A brilliant flash of genius might give you a story idea, but only through pure hard labour will you craft your tale to the final word. Ideally, you should write every day – writing emails and journal entries counts but if you only have an hour free at weekends, make that your writing time. Practise writing in same way as you would a sport or musical instrument.

Case study

Award-winning writer Kate DiCamillo (text) says that every day she hates the idea of having to write, but she doesn't let this stop her. Every day she writes her target two pages so she feels pleased with herself.

Now it's your turn

Brainstorm

Try this brainstorming exercise to unlock your imagination.

Sit quietly in your writing zone for a few moments. Close your eyes and take four long deep breaths. Then open your eyes. Set a stopwatch for two minutes.

Write the phrase 'Elementary, my dear Watson' at the top of a piece of paper and then, write down all the mystery words, phrases, names you first think of. Go, Go, GO! Don't think about it. Empty your brain!

❻ Reward yourself

Brilliant! You've proved you can write. Give yourself a gold star. Already you have found the key to your Secret Intelligence Files. And the more you practise like this, the more you will develop your powers of deduction.

TIPS AND TECHNIQUES

Brainstorming is your most important writer's tool. Like a set of keys it unlocks your Secret Intelligence Files; it sets your imagination free.
Keep all your brainstorming notes in a separate file or notebook. You will need them later.

❼ Read, read, read!

All good writing starts with good reading. There are many different kinds of mystery stories for you to choose from. So what makes a good mystery? Here are some well-tried formulae from classic mystery stories. Mystery stories have puzzles at their heart. These can involve robbery, kidnapping, murder, a disappearance, for example. There might be crimes committed for gain, or revenge, or even to protect a loved one. The mystery might be present day, historical or futuristic, involving supernatural happenings or international spies.

❽ See how characters are used

The central character usually uses their deductive powers to right wrongs and prove that crime does not pay. These must be people that readers meet in the story. There may be one or more main suspects, but their motives (reasons) for doing wrong must be believable. They must also have the opportunity and realistic means to carry out their crime.

❾ **Learn from the masters**

After the mystery is revealed, the story goes on to reconstruct the events
that explain it. Readers are given clues, which piece together like a jigsaw
to solve the mystery. Cunning writers may lay several red herrings or false
clues, but the ending must be both satisfying and surprising.
So, before you start writing, read as many different kinds
of mystery as possible. They won't all fit this mystery
blueprint, but find the ones that intrigue you most.
Look at how the writers drop clues. If a good
character starts to form in your mind,
make notes.

Now it's your turn

The hunt is on...

Write at the top of a new page in your notebook:
'The hunt is on'. In a two-minute practice jot down as
many different words and phrases you can think of that
mean searching and finding, e.g. detection, discovery,
turning up…

TIPS AND TECHNIQUES

*It's good to base your characters on people you know
or see – in the mall, on the bus, in the street.
Note facial details and odd quirks of behaviour.*

A WRITER'S VOICE

Great writers will help you find your own writer's 'voice'. First read a book for pleasure, but then go back to it. Interrogate it. Do the characters convince you? Do you like the ending? Were the clues cunningly laid? How is tension and suspense created?

❶ Finding your voice

Once you start reading as a writer you will notice that each story has its own rhythm and range of language that stays the same throughout the book. You will get to know different writers' styles. See that Richard Peck (author of *The Ghost Belonged to Me*) writes nothing like Edgar Allan Poe, or that Anthony Horowitz is poles apart from Conan Doyle. Every writer has a distinctive voice – one that your sleuthing mind will soon recognize.

❷ Experiment

Once you've found a writer or writers whose books you really enjoy, it's tempting to stick to them. Don't! You'll probably copy the way they write. Experiment. Mix and match. Reading a historical novel could give you all the background details you need for your own story.

Now it's your turn

How to find your voice

Pick an exciting scene from your favourite mystery book. Rewrite it as if you were there. Give yourself a leading role – either as sleuth or sleuthed.

WRITERS' VOICES

Look at the kinds of words these authors use. Do they use lots of adjectives? What about the length of their sentences? Which style do you prefer to read?

CONAN DOYLE

I had called upon my friend Sherlock Holmes...He was lounging upon the sofa...A lens and a forceps lying upon the seat of the chair suggested that the hat had been suspended in this manner for the purpose of examination.

Sir Arthur Conan Doyle, *The Adventure of the Blue Carbuncle*

CAROLYN KEENE

"Talk about sleazy. Look at this headline," Bess Marvin said indignantly, sliding Today's Times across the kitchen table to Nancy.
"The poor guy's dead, and all anyone can talk about is his money."

Carolyn Keene, *Nancy Drew: Make No Mistake*

ANTHONY HOROWITZ

Alex looked up and realized that everyone was staring at him. Mr Donovan had just asked him something. He quickly scanned the blackboard, taking in the figures. "Yes, sir," he said, "x equals seven and y is fifteen."
The maths teacher sighed. "Yes, Alex. You're absolutely right. But actually I was just asking you to open the window."

Anthony Horowitz, *Stormbreaker*

EDGAR ALLAN POE

During the whole of a dull, dark, and soundless day in the autumn of the year, when the clouds hung oppressively low in the heavens, I had been passing alone, on horseback, through the singularly dreary tract of country, and at length found myself, as the shades of evening drew on, within the view of the melancholy House of Usher.

Edgar Allan Poe, *The Fall of the House of Usher*

3 Look all around you

If you ask a writer where they get their story ideas, they will probably answer 'everywhere!' Finding a good mystery story depends on how you look at things. If you think your life is boring and nothing exciting happens, then you'll find it hard, but if you look at your world with fresh eyes, plenty of stories will crop up.

4 Play the part

A mystery story is a puzzle – something unusual that 'doesn't fit', something unexplained, something illegal or spooky. It could be happening right next door. Imagine you are a private eye waiting for some suspect to show up at a particular house in your street. Or you've seen an odd message in the 'Lost and Found' column of the local paper. Who's it for? Who might respond?

Focusing the mind

If you have binoculars, use them to look down your street, or sit in a shopping mall watching an area buzzing with activity. For 15 minutes log everything that happens there. Describe how people behave. That boy on the bench checking his watch, is he looking for his date or is there something more sinister going on? Take notes on his appearance – he could be a suspect. All the details you record could lead to a yarn, and you are learning a writer – detective's most essential skill – to study people and their behaviour. Ask why, how and what if? questions. What if the boy's dad is robbing a bank (above)?' And as soon as you ask questions, your imagination will start producing ideas.

❺ Use what you know

So to be a writer you must search inside your own head for ideas: break into those Secret Intelligence Files that you have tucked away in your subconscious mind – all the stories you've ever read, the TV shows you've watched such as the X-files (left), and all the facts you've ever learned. Brainstorming and scribbling down first thoughts is one way to start accessing all that story-making material.

TIPS AND TECHNIQUES

A story idea is only the start. To make it into a good story takes hard work and lots of thinking. Brainstorm when you are bored or nervous. Make lists. How many different ways can you describe how you're feeling? Bored as...concrete? Quivery as...a rat's tail?

MUGGLING REVIVAL.

How an Old-Time Trade is Returning to the South Coast.

uggling as carried on by our forefathers along the South Coast oppo-
site the French ports is again rampant, higher duties having led
To a widespread revival.
a the following special article a Customs officer, with an intimate ex-
perience of this part of the coast, describes from his own knowledge
the new style of smugglers and their methods.

By a Customs Officer.

❻ Read the newspapers

One sure-fire way to develop mystery story ideas is to study your local newspaper. Start a scrapbook collection of good stories: robberies, missing people, scandals over land development. Again, pose questions as you scan the paper. Highlight any interviews with real people expressing their views or feelings. All this will help you create your own characters.

❼ Get to the library

Your local library will probably also have old newspapers on microfilm. Perhaps there was some big crime story in the recent past that the librarian might help you to track down. Or maybe there is a local mystery – an eerie house or the unexplained disappearance of some rich recluse. Surf the Internet for ideas. The FBI Adventure site will give you some of their big case details, as well as access to a wealth of forensic details (www.fbi.gov). And of course, all those TV detective shows will give you lots of valuable information.

FBI ADVENTURE

FBI AGENTS INVESTIGATE CRIMES AROUND THE WORLD

Now it's your turn

Your dad is a bank robber!

Try developing the last writing exercise with your father as a bank robber, you will need all these kinds of human details to make a believable story.
You'll also need some technical information about break-ins. The criminology section in your library may have a book on famous bank robberies.
Or perhaps your fictional 'dad' devised a computer program that did the job instead, in which case, computer fraud is the topic to research.

Case study

"Elementary, my dear Watson!"
Sir Arthur Conan Doyle was a
doctor by profession. He trained at
Edinburgh University and there he
was much influenced by Professor
John Bell who used deductive
reasoning to diagnose disease.
Conan Doyle was so impressed by
his methods that he applied the
same principles when he created
Sherlock Holmes (left and below).

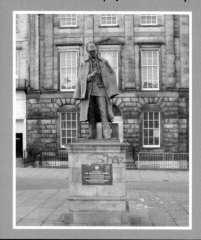

TIPS AND TECHNIQUES

Use your own technical knowledge for story settings.
If you have special skills or interests, then think how
you can use this specialist
knowledge. Or does someone
in your family have an interesting job or work in
a place that has plenty of scope for mystery?
These insights are real gifts for a writer. Use
them for all you are worth. When watching a
TV mystery, don't forget to make notes on any
useful technical information.

8 Discover a setting

Now you need to create your story's setting. You must find ways to make it believable and it needs to work for your story. If you haven't planned it properly, your hero could end up stuck forever in a blind alley, simply because they have no believable way out!

9 Drop hints

If particular places or artefacts are going to be crucial to solving the mystery, then their existence must be established early on in the story. They must be part of the landscape that the reader can picture, though not in an obvious way.

> 'What an eerie place! I stepped through the door and a huge grizzly attacked me – all teeth and claws. It took me a moment to realize he was stuffed, but by then I'd swung round into a huge urn, which teetered and rocked on its stand. I steadied it just before it fell on me. All round the walls, grim antique faces sneered down at me.'
>
> Tish Farrell

Suppose a large marble urn in an old lady's grand house is a possible murder weapon. Early on the readers need to see it – but not see it. One way to do this, is to mention it in a list of other things, perhaps when your hero goes to tea:Later, when a victim is found apparently crushed by the urn, readers will think they know exactly what happened. But was it an accident, or made to look like one? Or will it turn out to be just another red herring?

TIPS AND TECHNIQUES

When brainstorming, don't forget to write top-of-the-head thoughts. Don't be afraid to write nonsense. It can lead to brilliant stuff. If you want to have a historical setting for your mystery, make sure you know your facts.

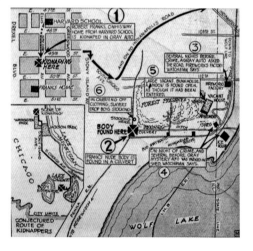

❿ Build a landscape

You can begin from a specific place and build the landscape around it, or work from a general landscape and zoom into a specific location later. You could draw a map of the area and use coloured stickers to highlight the location of each crime. If your setting is real, then think how the local transport routes, parks and landmarks might serve your story.

Now it's your turn

Be a real detective

It's time to do some legwork. Study places like the ones you want to use in your story. You could start with your own bedroom. Then there is your school, the museum, train station or park. Take a notebook. Imagine you're seeing the place for the first time. What do you notice: a particular smell or atmosphere; certain noises or textures? Each time do a two-minute brainstorm, noting five things you see, hear, feel and smell.

⑪ Picking details

Both new and experienced writers can fall into the trap of writing too much description. If it gets in the way of the story, then readers will skip it, or shut the book. The trick is to say just enough for readers to place your characters.

⑫ Scene setting recipe 1

If your hero, or hero's assistant, is the narrator, then their 'voice' will also help to capture readers' interest. Francis O'Roark Dowell's murder mystery, *Dovey Coe*, is set in rural North Carolina (right), and told from prime suspect Dovey's first person viewpoint. In the following extract, the description of setting is being used to tell us several things about Dovey. See how many separate pieces of information are stated or implied:

Every time I start complaining about having to walk a half mile down the mountain to school, I remember how lucky we are to own our land. It ain't much – four acres, a five-room house, and a barn – but it keeps us Coes from being beholden to Homer Caraway, and I'd walk ten miles to school to keep it that way.

Francis O'Roark Dowell, *Dovey Coe*

⑬ Scene setting recipe 2

Scene setting can be used to create mood, mystery and suspense from the opening line. At the start of *Big Mouth And Ugly Girl*, Joyce Carol Oates' scene setting is stark and ordinary, but she immediately introduces a mystery and hooks our curiosity:

It was an ordinary January afternoon, a Thursday, when they came for Matt Donaghy. They came for him in fifth period, which was Matt's study period, in room 220 of Rocky High School, Westchester County.

Joyce Carol Oates, *Big Mouth And Ugly Girl*

⑭ Scene setting recipe 3

There will be times in your story for straightforward scene setting, at which Enid Blyton excelled. In *Five on a Treasure Island*, she sums up Julian, Dick and Anne's first impression of their cousin's house in two sentences:

> *They liked it. It felt old and mysterious somehow, and the furniture was old and very beautiful.*
>
> Enid Blyton, *Five on a Treasure Island*

⑮ Scene setting recipe 4

Find ways to also trigger your readers' senses to make the scene more real. At the start of Charlie Higson's SilverFin, a boy is preparing to break in under a barbed wire fence to poach fish from the laird's estate. Extra tension is added, knowing that the boy will have to cross open ground:

> *The afternoon light was fading into evening, taking all the detail from the land with it. Here, on this side of the fence, among the thick gorse and juniper and low rowan trees, he was well hidden, but soon...soon he was going under the wire, and on the other side the tree cover quickly fell away.*
>
> Charlie Higson, *SilverFin*

Now it's your turn

Describe your hero's bedroom

Choose things that reflect your hero's character and reflect their interests and tastes.
What's under their pillow?
Where do they hide things?
What kinds of clothes are in the wardrobe?
Once you have done this, you should be able to picture your hero more clearly.

CHAPTER 3: CREATING CHARACTERS

HEROES

Whether you have one hero or more, they are the ones who solve the mystery. You must care about them as if they were good friends, and find ways to make readers care about them too. Avoid making them perfect: perfect people aren't interesting.

➊ Choose heroic qualities

Imagine meeting your hero. You like something about them straight away and you want to be friends. What do you especially admire? Find out as much as possible before you start your story. There may be something in their past that sets the mystery in motion.

➋ Inspiration from others

Base them on a classic detective but don't simply copy them. That would be plagiarism. Take some characteristics, adapt them and mix them with real people or other characters. For example, if you mixed a bit of Sherlock Holmes with a class swot you might end up with a character like Hermione (above right) in the *Harry Potter* books.

TIPS AND TECHNIQUES

Try searching through the phone book if you can't think of a good name for your hero.

❸ Create a clear profile

Describe your sleuth near the start of your story so readers don't set off imagining someone being tall and dark, and you later reveal them to be red-haired and weedy. You'll risk losing readers' good will. Your hero also needs a history. Make it brief, but make sure you remember what it is as you write the story.

❹ What's the problem

In *Dovey Coe*, Dovey is so likeable, it is hard to understand how she has been charged with murder. However, she does speak her mind, often in scathing terms. She also sets out to make a very public enemy of Parnell Caraway – *'I'd just as soon shoot him as look at him...'* she says. Later, this is used as evidence. But she tells us herself, *'I admit that's my biggest drawback, not thinking things through far enough.'*

Now it's your turn

On the record

Open a file on your hero. Make out an official report, which you can add to later as more ideas come to you. Begin by filling out the personal details: name, age, address, nationality, previous addresses, details of immediate relatives. Describe the hero's appearance, and any identifying characteristics. Give details of how they live and what they do. Do some sketches too, or cut out faces from magazines and newspapers.

❺ **What kind of villain?**

In a mystery, the villain (antagonist) must be present for a large portion of the story. When writing in a classic whodunnit style, you must make them visible, but not obvious. You could have a number of suspects who are eliminated one-by-one. Alternatively, your hero may know who the villain is, but can't prove it.

❻ **Why are they criminal?**

Before you start writing, find out what makes your villain bad. Are they a bully or hungry for power? Do they want money, revenge or a way out of a situation? Are they a victim of circumstance or just plain evil? Here Herod Sayle explains his motivation in *Stormbreaker*:

> *From the moment I arrived at the school, I was mocked and bullied. Because of my size. Because of the colour of my skin. Because I couldn't speak English well. Because I wasn't one of them. They had names for me. Herod Smell. Goat-boy. The Dwarf. They played tricks on me…My trousers ripped off me and hung out on the flagpole, underneath the Union Jack…*
>
> Anthony Horowitz, *Stormbreaker*

Case studies

Agatha Christie said she 'discovered' the murderer in her first detective story while in Torquay. He was dark and bearded (left) and just the kind of mysterious-looking character she needed to get her story going.

Villainous Profiles

Creating a good villain can make a mystery story so much more exciting. Here are some ideas for different types of baddies:

AN OBVIOUS VILLAIN

Dr Watson describes Dr Grimesby Roylott in The Adventure of the Blue Carbuncle *as he bursts into Sherlock Holmes' room –*

"A large face, seared with a thousand wrinkles, burned yellow with every passion…while his deepset, bile-shot eyes, and his high thin, fleshless nose, gave him he resemblance to a fierce old bird of prey." *It's a fitting description for a most devious killer.*

A MASTER CRIMINAL

In Stormbreaker, *Alex Rider's villain, Herod Sayle, is a corporate terrorist. He wants to take revenge on the prime minister, and on schoolchildren in general, because he was so tormented and bullied at school.*

AN UNUSUAL VILLAIN

In Wolf, *by Gillian Cross, the villain is a terrorist and someone unexpected too, but for much of the story we share Cassy's fearful sense of being stalked by an unknown terror.*

TRADING PLACES

In Dovey Coe *there's another kind of twist. We know in the first few lines that Parnell has been killed and Dovey charged with his murder – but the victim is the villain; and the hero is the only suspect.*

AN UNEXPECTED VILLAIN

In Zizou Corder's Lionboy, *Rafi Sadler is the young man who kidnaps Charlie Ashanti's scientist parents, and tries to kidnap Charlie too. He is known to all of them as a neighbour. Charlie even admires him a bit.*

TIPS AND TECHNIQUES

If you don't know what your villain looks like, do some people watching. Take your notebook. Play 20 Questions with your villain. Ask them 20 different things about themselves. See how much you can find out about them.

❼ The rest of the cast

Your sleuth will need people to discuss the case with, or to interact with in other ways, so you need some supporting characters. Scenes with minor characters are the best way to show the reader what your heroes are really like. You can show them being ingenious or sometimes being too clever and jumping to the wrong conclusion.

❽ Read famous examples

In Sherlock Holmes' stories, Dr Watson (right) is both assistant and narrator. This is a useful device. Dr Watson is often slow on the uptake and describes events at his own pace, not revealing Holmes' solution until the end. This way he builds suspense. If we knew things as soon as Holmes did, there would be less excitement and not much story.

❾ Build up relationships

The main characters in mysteries are often lonely, orphaned or isolated in some other way, but in *Dovey Coe*, the heroine Dovey is part of a loving family. This gives her a possible motive for killing Parnell because he wants to marry her sister, Caroline, and makes dark threats about sending their deaf brother, Amos, to an institution.

TIPS AND TECHNIQUES

Supporting characters (even dogs) must add to the story in some way. If they haven't a job to do, cut them out. The conversations between helpers and hero adds variety, interest, and are a good way of revealing the thought processes involved in solving the mystery.

Now it's your turn

Writing biographies

Choose five people who you know really well. They could be friends of the family or classmates. Make each one as fascinating as possible in no more than three sentences each.

⑩ Memorable characters

Supporting characters – helpers or suspects – will not be as developed as your hero, so you must find ways to fix them in your readers' minds. Be quick and interesting so they add to the story, not hold it up. Here we meet Herod Sayle's trusty assistant, Mr Grin, for the first time in *Stormbreaker*:

> *From a distance it looked as if he was smiling, but as he grew closer Alex gasped. The man had two horrendous scars, one on each side of his mouth, twisting all the way up to his ears. It was as if someone had attempted to cut his face in half.*
>
> Anthony Horowitz, *Stormbreaker*

⑪ Animal detectives?

Of course, your assistants may not all be human. You could include animals. The fifth member of Enid Blyton's *Famous Five* sleuthing team is a dog called Timmy.

WHO'S SPEAKING?

Before you can write your opening line, you must decide who is telling your story. Do you want to tell the readers everything, showing all the characters and how they are behaving or feeling? Do you want to tell one particular person's story or will another character tell their story?

❶ The first person

In detective stories, events are often described in the first person viewpoint. This instantly makes everything sound more believable, but it can only give that one person's observations. Sherlock Holmes' cases are all related by Dr. Watson shown at the beginning of *The Adventure of the Speckled Band*:

> *On glancing over my notes of the seventy-odd cases in which I have during the last eight years studied the methods of my friend Sherlock Holmes, I find many tragic, some comic, a large number merely strange, but none commonplace.*
>
> Sir Arthur Conan Doyle, *The Adventure of the Speckled Band*

❷ An all-seeing view

Nancy Drew stories are told from the all-seeing viewpoint. This is also called the objective view – you are not siding with one character or another – you can describe everything, but it is less personal or involving than other viewpoints.

> *Matt whirled round to face Nancy. "What are you doing here?" he asked. Ignoring Matt, Nancy said to Jake Loomis, "Let Bess go." Bess's eyes were wide with fear, and she was trembling. Her arm was twisted painfully behind her, but Loomis didn't release his grip.*
>
> Carolyn Keene, *Nancy Drew: Make No Mistake*

❸ The third person

The third person viewpoint tells the story as if the camera was inside the head of one particular character. You can't reveal other characters' thoughts or feelings, except through dialogue. The viewpoint character can also guess from observation, but they might not get it right! They can't talk about things they haven't seen, not unless another character has given them the information – for example:

> *It was only later that he learned the whole truth. It was Inspector Parker who told him. He said that the forger had made the tiniest error...*
>
> Tish Farrell

❹ The multiple person

In short stories, it is usual to stick to one character's viewpoint, but novels sometimes use several or multiple third person viewpoints. Using several viewpoints can add drama: one character's view of events might be very different from another's. You can also choose to switch viewpoints at a cliffhanger – when something dangerous or exciting is about to happen.

Now it's your turn

Changing views...

Write a short scene: your hero is pursuing the villain. First write from the all-seeing viewpoint. Describe the behaviour of both characters. Then re-write it in the third person, giving only your hero's viewpoint of the pursuit. Finally, write in the first person as if you are the hero. Read your efforts aloud to yourself. Which one do you prefer and why?

READY TO WRITE

When your story starts simmering in your mind, it's a good idea to write brief account of it. Write down what you would say if someone asked you 'What's it about then?' This is called a synopsis. A good synopsis will get your work read. But don't give away the ending!

❶ Back cover inspiration

Visit the library or a bookshop to look at as many mystery books as you can. Read the blurbs: the publishers' information on the back. See how it says just enough to make you want to read the book. The back cover of The Ruby in the Smoke, by Philip Pullman, captures the reader's interest from the first sentence:

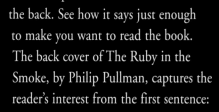

Sally Lockhart is sixteen, an orphan, and she's just struck a man dead. Not with a weapon, though she has a pistol, and probably the heart to use it. Sally killed Mr Higgs with just three words – The Seven Blessings. Unfortunately, she still has no idea what they mean, and why her drowned father's colleague dies of fear when he heard them...

❷ Fine-tune your theme

At the same time you might like to think about your story's theme. What is the central idea? This will shape your villain's motives for committing the crime, but will only be revealed in your detective's final solution.

Write your blurb

Sum up your own story in a single striking sentence; two at most. Then introduce the hero and outline the main action in no more than three short paragraphs. Don't give away the ending!

❸ Create a synopsis

Novelists often list all their chapters before they start writing, and say briefly what will happen in each one. This is called a chapter synopsis. It provides the mystery writer with a skeleton plot which helps to keep their story on track.

❹ Make a story map

Now you have a synopsis that says what your story is about. You have a cast of characters and a setting, and you know from whose viewpoint you wish to tell the tale. The last thing you need before you start, is a story map. Before film-makers can start filming, they must know the main story episodes and decide how they can best tell their story in filmed images. To help them, they map out the plot (the sequence of events) in a series of sketches called storyboards. You can do this for your story. Draw the main episodes in pictures. Add a few notes that say what is happening in each scene.

TIPS AND TECHNIQUES

If when you've written a synopsis, you find a flaw in your story, then rethink the synopsis; don't try writing the story in the hopes that no one else will notice the problem. They will!

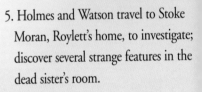

❺ Get inspiration from a classic

Here are some storyboard captions for *The Adventure of the Speckled Band* by Sherlock Holmes:

1. Helen Stoner arrives at Holmes' rooms, saying she's afraid for her life.

2. Tells Holmes about the mysterious death of her twin sister and her dying words about a speckled band.

3. Gives some family history and tells of her violent stepfather Dr. Roylett who controls the money left her by her mother.

4. After she leaves, Dr Roylett bursts in and threatens Holmes if he starts interfering.

5. Holmes and Watson travel to Stoke Moran, Roylett's home, to investigate; discover several strange features in the dead sister's room.

6. Later they go secretly to spend the night in the room, and Holmes warns Watson of the grave danger.

7. In the night, Holmes raises the alarm, lashing out with his cane.

8. A scream comes from Dr. Roylott's room. They find him dead with a speckled band round his head.

9. Holmes explains the case to Watson.

TIPS AND TECHNIQUES

Don't let a novel's length put you off from starting one. If you use the story map approach it is often easier to write a novel than it is to write a good short story.

❻ Write a novel?

Novels have beginnings, middles and ends just like short stories, but the stories themselves are more complex. They have more details, more character development, and subplots. The chapters make the storytelling manageable. Each one has a beginning, middle and end, like a mini-story inside the larger one, but it also carries the story forward, adding more mystery and creating more and more suspense.

To turn the short story The Adventure of the Speckled Band into a novel, look at each scene caption and think how to make it into an episode that shows readers more about the characters and their problems. Chapter 1 could start with Helen Stoner waking in terror, then flying to London to seek help. You could show all the difficulties she has leaving the house secretly. A novel, then, is not a short story made longer, but a short story made fatter. The suspense is built up from chapter to chapter, and any mysteries spun out so that readers are drawn more deeply into the story.

Now it's your turn

Weave a story web

If you're still struggling to come up with a plot for your mystery, get a large piece of paper. In the centre draw a rough sketch of your hero. Put them inside a circle. As you are drawing, imagine that you are that hero, looking outside the circle, trying to solve a riddle. Then draw six spokes from your hero circle. Each spoke leads to an empty circle. In one minute, without thinking at all, write in each circle one thing that you have discovered. It can be an object or a piece of information – the dog didn't bark; all the doors and windows were locked at the crime scene; a torn up plane ticket…The wilder your thoughts, the more likely they will lead to something you can use.

❼ Create an intriguing beginning

Mystery stories should begin with a mystery. An intriguing first sentence is a good start. Readers must know at once that there will be unusual riddles to solve. But a mystery story is also about people and the heroes will have their own problems, or at least some very pressing reason to solve the mystery.

❽ Hook your reader

At the start of your story, you bait your hook with the tastiest titbits, so the reader bites. But you also must lay solid foundations, so that as you build your story, you end up with something strong. It is therefore essential that you know your mystery story's ending before you start writing. Then you can work backwards, dropping hints and clues in advance. This is called foreshadowing and it is an important storytelling tool.

Case study

Wilkie Collins (below) said this about how to treat readers: Make 'em laugh, make 'em cry, make 'em wait.

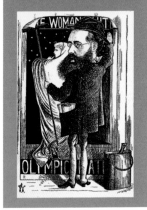

Now it's your turn

Good beginnings

Write the opening scene of your story. Introduce the hero and the mystery.
If possible, include some action. Look at ways to hook readers' interest and curiosity.
Or be spooky. Also decide if there's any important information that needs to be slipped in at this point. When you have finished, go back and concentrate on your first sentence.
Is it as exciting as you can make it?

❾ Make a good start

For good beginnings, create suspense, make the hero engaging and set the tone, whether it's dramatic, spooky, humorous or chilling. Here are two examples:

> *My name is Dovey Coe, and I reckon it don't matter is you like me or not. I'm here to lay the record straight, to let you know them folks saying I done terrible things are liars. I aim to prove it, too. I hated Parnell Caraway as much as the next person, but I didn't kill him.*

Frances O' Roark Dowell, *Dovey Coe*

> *'The boy crept up to the fence and looked around. There was the familiar sign… KEEP OUT! PRIVATE PROPERTY. TRESPASSERS WILL BE SHOT.*
>
> *And hanging next to it, just to make sure that the message was clearly understood, were the bodies of several dead animals. Strung up like criminals, wire twisted round their broken necks.'*

Charlie Higson, *SilverFin*

TIPS AND TECHNIQUES

To learn how to write smack-in-the-eye first sentences, go to the library and read as many as possible. Make a note of your favourites. Story beginnings introduce the mystery, the hero investigator, and start the quest.

⑩ Build the tension

Once your sleuth is hot on the trail of mystery solving, you need to think about building up the excitement bit by bit until you reach the climax of your story. So don't put all your most thrilling action in the opening scenes. Save the best till last.

⑪ Investigate the suspects

In most criminal investigations there are likely to be several suspects. Intrigue your readers by building a good case against each one. This will require all your mystery writer's cunning. Both sleuth and readers must believe that every suspect is a real possibility – or at least until some new clue gives them a watertight alibi.

⑫ Add complications

Send your sleuth off on their quest, and then make things really tough. For example, in Zizou Corder's *Lionboy*, hero Charlie stows away on a circus ship to find his kidnapped parents. The chase is hard enough, but once on board, he agrees to rescue some lions from their cruel trainer. Now he has to dodge his pursuers, reach Venice, and all with six large lions depending on him.

⑬ Add a false ending

Your case is cracked. The prime suspect is in jail. But just as your hero is set to close their casebook, another crime is committed – the same pattern as before, but much more evil or shocking. Now it's time to track down the real culprit, but can your hero measure up this time?

⑭ Add the time factor

If your sleuth is time challenged, you instantly add drama. Perhaps they must find evidence to clear a client before a court case closes, or track down the real culprit before they flee the country, or commit another crime.

Now it's your turn

Flaws and weaknesses

A hero's flaws and weaknesses can add complications to a mystery story? For example, a vivid imagination might cause them to jump to the wrong conclusions, or a grudge might make them think an old enemy is guilty when they aren't. In five minutes brainstorm your first thoughts about your own hero's weaknesses. How can they make your story more exciting?

TIPS AND TECHNIQUES

To make the middle of your story gripping, add complications and twists. Pile on the challenges. Lay false trails. Give your sleuth a hard time.

15 Dramatic climaxes

Finding a good ending is the hardest part of writing a mystery. As the writer, you will know 'whodunnit' right from the start. You will also have worked hard to lay all the necessary clues as the story unfolds. But when the final piece of the jigsaw is put in place, readers must be both surprised at your solution and satisfied that you haven't cheated them.

16 Tie up loose ends

All the false trails of your story middle must now come to an exciting climax. The conflicts must be resolved with no niggling loose ends. And your hero must have learned or changed in some way. Mystery story endings are usually concerned with wrongs being righted. Some have a final cunning twist; others end with some dry humour. Most endings aim to be hopeful rather than completely happy.

17 Use humour

Sherlock Holmes often has a wry comment to make as he concludes his investigations. In *The Adventure of the Speckled Band*, the wicked Dr Grimesby Roylott (far right) meets a just end after murdering one stepdaughter and attempting to murder a second. He is killed by the venomous snake that he has trained to crawl down a bell-pull into his stepdaughter's bedroom. Holmes foils the attempt. At the end, he admits to Watson that the blows of his cane drove the reptile back to attack its owner:

In this way I am no doubt indirectly responsible for Dr Grimesby Roylott's death, and I cannot say that it is likely to weigh very heavily upon my conscience.

Sir Arthur Conan Doyle, *The Adventure of the Speckled Band*

TIPS AND TECHNIQUES

Study TV mysteries such as Inspector Morse. Think about beginnings, middles and ends. Take notes!

⑱ Suggest a new beginning

Good story endings often refer in some way to the beginning of the story. This will remind readers where the tale started and make the point that something important has changed. At the start of Malorie Blackman's *Hacker*, Vicky and her brother, Gib, do not seem to get on at all. For one thing Vicky is adopted. But at the end, they reach an understanding that shows readers how things have changed and not changed! Gib persuades Vicky to come home with one of his usual backhanded remarks. Vicky surrenders, but in her own wry way: *'That's my brother. Sometimes he can be a right toe-rag and a half!'*

Bad endings are ones that:

• Trick readers by springing a totally surprise solution;

• Simply fizzle out;

• Fail to show how the characters have changed in some way;

• Are too grim and leave the reader with no hope.

Now it's your turn

Choose your own ending

Can you think of another ending to your favourite mystery story? Could someone else have committed the crime? If so, why not write it? Go back and read both versions later to see which you prefer. Use your own ending to write another story.

MAKING WORDS WORK

Writing with bite means using words wisely. The scene should be set as quickly as possible by choosing the most striking details. Mix with action to keep your readers hooked.

❶ Use words wisely

Here is the opening setting from Leon Garfield's historical ghost and murder mystery, The Empty Sleeve. Notice the strong first sentence hook. His description of the weather sets the tone:

> *It takes all sorts to make a world, but only one to unmake it. On a well-remembered Saturday morning in January, when the air was murderous with wind and snow, like a madman made of feathers, a solitary old man trudged along a street in Rotherhithe, battered, blinded and bewildered by the weather.*
>
> Leon Garfield, *The Empty Sleeve*

Is there a single word in the Leon Garfield extract that you would like to leave out? Read your own work aloud too. You will soon hear where you have written a rambling sentence with too many adjectives.

❷ Paint pictures with words

Another way to quickly bring scenes alive for readers is to use imagery. In Dovey Coe, Dovey describes a scene in winter using a simile – Now the trees…stand dusted in white, and it looks like they got ghosts dancing through their branches. A simile is when you say something is like something else.

TIPS AND TECHNIQUES

A metaphor is when you say a man is a fox, meaning that he's dishonest; a simile is when you say something is like something else: he moves like a fox.

❸ Vary the mood

If a story stays in the same mood from start to finish, it's less interesting. Anthony Horowitz (left) is brilliant at orchestrating suspense – building to climaxes with high-octane action, then giving readers some light relief with quieter moments that are a welcome break from the drama.

❹ Change the rhythm

Changing the rhythm and length of your sentences is another way to keep readers reading. Action scenes should focus on what is happening. But if you are building up for something scary, spin out the phrases, adding pauses and detail that make the scene more real; imagine yourself sneaking up on your reader; build the tension and…then strike!

Now it's your turn

Try some word play

Cut up scrap paper into at least sixty small squares. Brainstorm thirty adjectives and thirty nouns. Or use a thesaurus, dictionary or any large book and pick them out at random. Write one word on each square and keep the nouns and adjectives separate. Then keep dealing yourself one from each pile. See what pairs you get.

TALL monstrosities TREE ingenious WALLS FAMISHED

CREATING DIALOGUE

Dialogue plays a big part in many mystery stories. In the Nancy Drew and Hardy Boys books, dialogue often carries the plot. Past and present events, puzzling over clues and solutions are all reported in conversations between the Hardy Boys and other characters. Dialogue must flow smoothly and sound just right.

❶ Fictional eavesdropping

The best way to learn about dialogue is to switch on your listening ear and eavesdrop. Tune into people's conversations. Pay attention to rhythm and turns of phrase.
Watch people's body language too when they are whispering or arguing. Remember, all the great sleuths are students of human behaviour and naturally nosy.

LOOK, LISTEN, ABSORB…

Now it's your turn

Discussing the evidence

Study the dialogue in a Nancy Drew or Hardy Boys book. Write a short scene in your own story where your sleuth is discussing something with a friend or assistant. Show them discussing 'the evidence' – do they disagree or come up with solutions? What do they decide to do next?

❷ Following convention

Written dialogue follows certain conventions or rules. It is usual to start a new paragraph with every new speaker. What they say is enclosed in inverted commas, followed by speech tags – 'he said' or 'she said' – to indicate the speaker. There may be other information too. Notice that speech tags are left out in the exchanges when it is clear who is speaking. Here's some dialogue from Nancy Drew:

> *"Where do we start?" George asked.*
> *"Well, I'd like to check out Gary Page's credentials at the Chicago Clarion," Nancy suggested.*
> *George looked at her watch. "If we leave right now, we could be back by early evening."*
> *"Well, I already believe Matt," Bess said. "But if it'll make you guys feel better, let's go."*
> *Nancy frowned. "I wish I had a photo of him to take with us, to show to the people at the paper."*
> *"No problem," said Bess, blushing a little. "I just happen to have a very recent picture of him."*
> *She fumbled in her purse and drew out an instant photo of Matt.*
> *"Where did you get that?" Nancy and George asked at the same time.'*
>
> Carolyn Keene, *Make No Mistake: Nancy Drew*

In fiction, if a speaker stumbles, it is only suggested with the occasional 'um' or 'er' or three dots or some stammered words. Dialogue doesn't copy natural speech. It gives an edited impression of how people speak.

TIPS AND TECHNIQUES

When writing dialogue, don't just stick to 'said'. Words like 'asked' and 'replied' add variety.

❸ Give subtle information

In Anthony Horowitz's *Stormbreaker*, Alan Blunt of MI6 tells Alex Rider that they need his help. He explains why:

> *"Have you heard of a man called Herod Sayle?" Alex thought for a moment. "I've seen his name in the newspapers. He's something to do with computers. And he owns racehorses. Doesn't he come from somewhere in Egypt?"*
>
> *"No. Lebanon." Blunt took a sip of wine. "Let me tell you his story, Alex. I'm sure you'll find it of interest…"*
>
> *Herod Sayle was born in complete poverty in the back streets of Beirut…"*
>
> Anthony Horowitz, *Stormbreaker*

Blunt then goes on to give the villain's life history. Horowitz needs readers and Alex to know this information. The rest of the story depends on it. He could have written it as narrative, but then we might have skipped it. Instead, to make sure we don't, he writes it as part of a conversation. Like Alex, we 'listen' with attention.

❹ Show, don't tell

Dialogue is a very useful storytelling tool. The Nancy Drew and Hardy Boys (right) stories are told from the all-seeing viewpoint, and so using dialogue saves having to say what people are thinking. We simply hear their views in swift, short exchanges, which is very useful in the mystery story genre where there is a lot of deductive reasoning: Nancy suddenly remembered something. This made her think of another odd incident. She'd not taken much notice of it at the time, but now she began to wonder…How much better to have her exclaim:

> *"Hey, wait a minute, Dad, the witness has to be lying. I've just remembered. George said she saw her downtown. So she couldn't have been at the house when she said she was…"*
>
> Carolyn Keene, *Make No Mistake: Nancy Drew*

Now it's your turn

The art of speech writing

Think about a scene in your story where something quite complicated needs to be explained – some event, or something in a character's history that has made them act in a certain way. Choose people who are likely to sound different from one another, say an adult and a child. Make them sound angry, disappointed, frightened or hurt.

❺ Break up the narrative

Dialogue is used to break up blocks of narrative (storytelling), and give readers' eyes a rest. It adds variety and pace too. Good dialogue is quicker to read and conveys information more quickly than descriptive prose.

❻ Maintain the pace

Characters do not make idle chitchat. Whatever they say will convey information – about themselves, other characters and what is happening. You can use it to reveal their history, or to drop hints that foreshadow dangers ahead. You can show characters lying and misleading other characters. Or you can make characters give themselves away.

Good dialogue...

- Conveys information
- Reveals character
- Advances the story

CREATING DIALOGUE

❼ Make characters sound different to you

Have imaginary conversations with your characters. Try to hear their voice in your head. Here are some varied examples:

❽ Class

Here is Dovey Coe wondering why her lawyer is doing charity work in taking her case. He replies:

❾ Cold characters

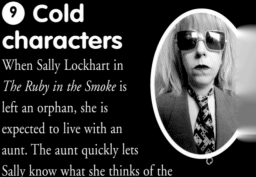

When Sally Lockhart in *The Ruby in the Smoke* is left an orphan, she is expected to live with an aunt. The aunt quickly lets Sally know what she thinks of the arrangement. She sounds a cold-hearted, but dutiful Victorian English lady:

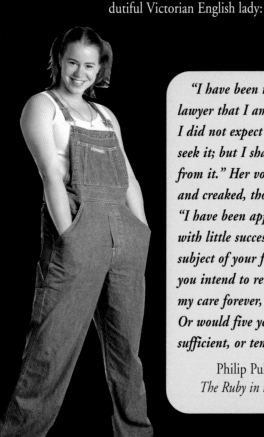

"I feel it is part of my job to defend those who can't afford an expensive private attorney. In fact, that is one of the reasons I went into the law. Liberty and justice for all…"

"…They must pay you a sight of money for you to afford a suit like that."

"No, Miss Dovey," he said, opening his brief case. "They don't pay me much at all. You certainly speak your mind, don't you?"

Frances O'Roark Dowell,
Dovey Coe

"I have been told by my lawyer that I am your aunt. I did not expect it; I did not seek it; but I shall not shrink from it." Her voice whined and creaked, thought Sally. "I have been applying myself with little success to the subject of your future. Do you intend to remain under my care forever, I wonder? Or would five years be sufficient, or ten?"

Philip Pullman,
The Ruby in the Smoke

⑩ Speak with shock

In Joyce Carol Oates' *Big Mouth And Ugly Girl*, Matt is taken by detectives to see the headmaster and is accused of trying to blow up his school:

> *Matt's teeth were chattering. He tried to speak calmly.*
> *"Look, this is crazy. I never...what you're saying?"*
> *"We've had a report, Matt. Two reports. Two witnesses. They heard you."*
> *"Heard me...what?"*
> *"Threaten to 'blow up the school'."*
> *Matt stared at the detective, uncomprehending.*
> *"Threaten to 'massacre' as many people as you could. In the school cafeteria, just a few hours ago. Are you denying it?"*
> *"Y-yes! I'm denying it."*
> *"You're denying it."*
> *"I think this is all crazy."*
> *"'This is all crazy.' That's your response?"*

Joyce Carol Oates, *Big Mouth And Ugly Girl*

Now it's your turn

A family conversation

Write down a typical conversation between you and one of your parents. Try to capture exactly how they speak. What words or phrases do they habitually use that are different from yours? Re-write it with a grandparent or elderly aunt speaking. Now think how your parents speak to their elders. Are there more differences?

BEATING WRITER'S BLOCK

When words dry up this is called writer's block. If you have been doing plenty of brainstorming exercises, you will already know the antidote to the main cause of writer's block – your Internal Critic, the real villain of the piece.

❶ Beating insecurities

Whenever your Internal Critic rears up, do a timed brainstorming exercise to cut it down to size. Write something positive: about your favourite things or a happy time.

❷ Find fresh ideas

There are other causes of writer's block. One is thinking that you have no ideas.

But as you have seen previously, ideas are everywhere. The trick is to stop panicking and sit quietly. Any of the exercises in this book will trigger some creative thoughts.

TIPS AND TECHNIQUES

All stories have their natural time to emerge. If you get stuck with one, start another and go back to it later. You won't run out of ideas if you keep reading. But remember to write your ideas down.

❸ Responding to criticism

No one enjoys rejection or criticism, but it is an important part of learning to be a writer. If you invite someone to read your stories, you have to prepare yourself for negative comments. As you develop your writing skills, you will develop faith in yourself. You will see rejection as a chance to re-write your story, if it really needs it.

❹ Don't stall!

Another problem is stalling half way through a story. This can be very depressing. But when it happens, it's often because you haven't thought the story through properly. If it happens to you, try the following exercise; it is a variation of the one on page 35.

Now it's your turn

How to kick-start your story

In the middle of a large sheet of paper, draw your hero inside a circle. Imagine that hero is you. Think about the mystery that you want to solve. Now draw six spokes round your hero circle. Each leads to another circle. Inside each one sketch a different scene, or write it as notes. Each circle will be some new course of action that you might take, or some obstacle that an enemy sets in your path. Give yourself 20 minutes. You may be surprised how the story starts growing.

❺ Understanding writer's block

The kind of writer's block that leaves you stuck mid-story, usually means there has not been enough planning. Maybe some horrible flaw in your plot has cropped up and looks like ruining everything. Don't panic! There will be an answer.

❻ Group brainstorming

If a key character (hero or villain) isn't coming to life, do some group brainstorming. Start by writing a brief character description at the top of a sheet of paper. When two minutes are up, pass it to a friend to add their ideas to yours. Don't worry about complete sentences. Thoughts are what count. Keep passing the paper round – the more friends willing to join in, the more ideas you will have. Mull over the results. Have you learned something about your character that you didn't know before?

❼ Compose a group story

Decide among you what the crime or mystery will be. Then everyone writes a character idea on a piece of paper, and drops it into a hat. Each person picks out a character at random and is responsible for developing that character and weaving them into the story. Did they commit the crime? What was their motive? Did they have the means and opportunity? To start, sit in a circle and take it in turns to develop the story. There are two rules: Speak your first thoughts and don't mind if others improve on your ideas. This is not about being clever. It's about shaping a story. The end result will be like a chapter synopsis, which you can develop later, either singly or together. But don't forget the all important story ingredients – problems, conflict and resolution.

Now it's your turn

Keep a journal

Write about life at school or home, record all the details of your hobbies and interests. Set yourself a minimum target length for each entry, say 300 words. If you use a computer for writing, you can count them easily. Make a note.
Never write less than your target, even if it means describing the pattern on your bedroom wallpaper or what's in your sandwich. But try to write more.
And look for ways of turning the day's events into an anecdote. Did your best friend have a row with her parents? Write about it. Write how you would feel if you were them.

❽ Use the news

Choose an interesting photo from a newspaper. If it's a place, make it the scene of the mystery. If it's a person, make them the subject of the mystery. Perhaps they have disappeared or been kidnapped. Pass the photo round the group. Everyone has to add their ideas about what has happened. Work out who did it, with what, why and how.

TIPS AND TECHNIQUES

If all else fails to spark inspiration and break that writer's block do something completely different. Walk the dog, clean out your bedroom. Doing tasks that give your mind a rest could be just the thing to spring an idea.

PREPARING YOUR WORK

When your story has been 'resting' in your desk for at least two weeks, take it out, and read it through. You will be able to read it with fresh eyes. Replace weak words with stronger ones. Simplify any rambling sentences.

❶ Editing

Read your work aloud. This will help you to simplify rambling sentences and correct dialogue that doesn't flow. Would a serious villain really say 'Yeh, whatever.' Cut out all unnecessary adjectives and adverbs and words like 'very'. This will instantly make your writing crisper. Think about the story, too. Does it have a satisfying end? Has the hero resolved the conflict in the best way? Does the end link with the beginning, and has your hero learned something and changed? When your story is as good as can be, write it out afresh or type it up on a computer. This is your manuscript.

❷ Think of a title

It is important to think up a good title; choose something intriguing and eye catching. Think about some titles you know and like.

TIPS AND TECHNIQUES

Canadian writer, Robert J. Sawyer suggests using the search facility on a computer to track down 'ly' followed by a space. It'll highlight all the adjectives you may want to remove. 'Really' will come up too, and can often go. You can repeat the exercise with 'very'. This simple editing alone will make your text much crisper.

❸ Be professional

If you have a computer, you can word process your manuscript and give it a professional presentation. Manuscripts should always be printed on one side of A4 white paper, with wide margins and double spacing. Pages should be numbered, and new chapters should start on a new page.

❹ Make your own book

If your school has its own publishing lab, why not use it to 'publish' your own story or make a class story anthology (collection). A computer will let you choose your own font (print style) or justify the text (making even length margins like a printed page). When you have typed and saved your story to a file, you can edit it quickly with the spell- and grammar checker, or move sections of your story around using the 'cut and paste' facility, which saves a lot of rewriting. Having your story on a computer file also means you can print a copy whenever you need one, or revise the whole story if you want to.

❺ Design a cover

Once your story is in good shape, you can print it out and then use the computer to design the cover. A graphics program will let you scan and print your own artwork, or download ready-made graphics. Or you could use your own digital photographs and learn how to manipulate them on screen to produce some highly original images. You can use yourself or friends as 'models' for your story's heroes.

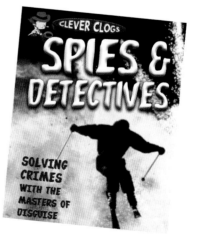

CLEVER CLOGS
SPIES & DETECTIVES
SOLVING CRIMES WITH THE MASTERS OF DISGUISE

❻ Some places to publish your story

The next step is to find an audience for your mystery-fiction work. Family members or classmates may be receptive. Or you may want to get your work published via a publishing house or online site. There are magazines and a number of writing websites that accept stories and novel chapters from young writers. Some give writing advice too and run regular competitions. Each site has its own rules about submitting work to them, so make sure you read them carefully before you send in a story. See page 62 for more details. You can also:

- Send things to your school magazine, or if your school doesn't have a magazine, then start your own with like-minded friends;

- Keep your eyes peeled when reading your local newspaper or your favourite comics and magazines. They might be running a writing competition that you can submit something to;

- Send it to a magazine or book publisher

❼ Writing clubs

Starting a writing club or critique group and exchanging stories is a great way of getting your mystery-fiction stories out there. It will also get you used to criticism from others, which will prove invaluable in learning how to write. Your local library might be kind enough to provide a forum for such a club.

Case study

Malorie Blackman used to work in the computer business, and her expert knowledge is reflected in her first novel Hacker. It took two years of publishers' rejection letters before it was accepted, and she nearly gave up the idea of writing. But now she says: 'Thank goodness I don't know when to admit defeat.'

⑧ Finding a publisher

Secure any submission with a paperclip and always enclose a short letter (saying what you have sent) and a stamped, addressed envelope for the story's return.

Study the market and find out which publishing houses are most likely to publish mystery fiction. Addresses of publishing houses and information about whether they accept submissions can be found in writers' handbooks. Bear in mind that manuscripts that haven't been asked for or paid for by a publisher – unsolicited submissions – are rarely published.

⑨ Don't despair!

Getting published is not the only thing! Being able to make up a story is a gift, so why not give yours to someone you love? Read it to a younger brother or sister. Tell it to your grandmother. Find your audience.

⑩ Writer's tip

Through stories we can explore all the good and bad things that make us human. This is what storytelling is about. It gives us hope. It shows us new possibilities. It makes us endlessly curious – to see what else we can discover and learn.

TIPS AND TECHNIQUES

READ, READ, READ, WRITE, WRITE, WRITE.

It's the only writing spell you will ever need.

WHEN YOU'VE FINISHED YOUR STORY

Finishing your first story, whether it is a short story or a whole novel, is a brilliant achievement. You have ransacked your Secret Intelligence Files and created something entirely new. But what next?

TOP SECRET

❶ Off on a tangent?

Perhaps while you were writing the first story, an idea started simmering in your mind. Perhaps you made a few notes in your 'ideas' file. Do those ideas still excite you? Go back to the start of this book and repeat some of the brainstorming exercises to help you develop the idea further.

❷ How about a sequel?

When thinking about your next work, ask yourself: 'Is there more to tell about the characters I have created? Is my hero now hooked on solving mysteries? Can I write a sequel or follow-up story? Is there a minor character whose tale I'm burning to tell?'

Mystery stories lend themselves to series. If you have created a cracking hero-sleuth, then they are bound to want to xunravel more mysteries. Readers like series, too. They become intrigued with a particular investigator's methods. Sherlock Holmes, Miss Marple, Hercule Poirot, Nancy Drew, the Hardy Boys, the Famous Five, Trixie Beldon, Encyclopaedia

Brown or the Box Car Children – they all have their following. Their fans try to beat them to their mystery's solution, or at least hope to learn more about these often enigmatic puzzle-solvers?

❸ Title task

While your story is 'resting', now is a good time to think of a title. Thinking of a snappy story title is another way of hooking your readers. For a mystery book, it's important that it's intriguing and eyecatching. Think about some titles you know or study the titles on the library shelves to get some ideas.

Now it's your turn

No one ever said writing was easy!

Write the above sentence at the top of a page and think about it for a few moments. Then brainstorm for five minutes. Write two lists – all the things you find difficult about writing and all the things you love about it. Now look over your writing problems. Consider them honestly. Are these things that can be fixed with more time, practice and more reading? Is learning to write more important to you than those problems? If the answer is yes, then give yourself five gold stars. Your stories will get written.

back story – the history of people or events that happened before the actual story begins

chapter synopsis – an outline saying briefly what is to happen in each chapter

cliffhanger – ending a chapter or switching viewpoint stories at a nail-biting moment

dramatic irony – the reader knows something the characters don't; it could be scary!

editing – removing all unnecessary words from your story and making it the best shape it can be

editor – the person who works in a publishing house and finds new books to publish. They also advise authors on how to improve their storytelling methods by telling them what needs adding or cutting

first person viewpoint – stories told in the first person and describing only what that person experiences – 'I saw…and 'I felt…'

foreshadowing – dropping hints of coming events or dangers that are essential to the outcome of the story

genre – a particular type of fiction, e.g. fantasy, historical, adventure, science fiction are all examples of different genres

internal critic – the voice that constantly criticises your work and makes you want to give up writing

list – the list of book titles that a publisher has already published or is about to publish

manuscript – your story when it is written down, either typed or by hand

metaphor – calling a man 'a mouse' is a metaphor. It is a word picture. From it we learn in one word that the man is timid or pathetic, not that he is actually a mouse

motivation – the reason why a character does something

narrative – the telling of the story

plagiarism – copying someone else's work and passing it off as your own; it is a serious offence

plot – the sequence of events that drives a story forwards; the problems that the hero must resolve

point of view (POV) – the eyes through which a story is told

publisher – a person or company who pays for an author's manuscript to be printed as a book and who distributes and sells that book

sequel – a story that carries an existing one forward

simile – saying something is like something else. It is a word picture, e.g. clouds liked frayed lace

synopsis – a short summary that describes what a story is about and introduces the main characters

theme – the main issue that the story addresses, e.g. good versus evil, how power corrupts, the importance of truth. A story can have more than one theme

third person viewpoint – stories told in the third person which only show events from that character's viewpoint, e.g. *Jem's heart leapt in his throat. Oh no! he thought. He'd been dreading this moment for months*

unsolicited submission – sending a book or story to a publishers without them asking you to. These submissions usually end up in 'the slush pile', a pile of manuscripts that are rarely read by editors.

writer's block – when writers think they can no longer write, or have used up all their ideas

Further information

You can learn a lot from famous mystery writers' websites. Look up your favourite writers. The late Joan Lowery Nixon has lots of useful advice on writing mysteries and a story example at: www.teacher.scholastic.com/writewit/mystery/read.htm

To learn more about mysteries and mystery writing check out:

www.kids.mysterynet.com/solveit and www.mysterynet.com and other mystery sites listed on webtech.kennesaw.edu/jcheek3/mysteries.htm

For specialist information and story ideas try the FBI Kids site at: www.fbi.gov/kids/6th12th/adventure/adventure.htm

For general writing advice see:

Author Aaron Shepherd's site: www.aaronshep.com/storytelling/
Writers' Tool Kit at www.channel4.com/learning/microsites/B/bookbox/writerstoolkit/home1.htm

Ask for a subscription to magazines such as *Cricket* and *Cicada* for your birthday. Or find them in your library. They publish the very best in young people's short fiction and you can learn your craft and read great stories at the same time. *Cicada* also accepts submissions from its subscribers. www.cricketmag.com

Make a good friend of your local librarian. They can direct you to useful sources of information that you might not have thought of. They will also know of any published author scheduled to speak in your area.

Places to submit your stories

The magazine *Stone Soup* accepts stories and artwork from 8- to 13-year-olds. Their website is www.stonesoup.com

The *Young Writers Club* is an Internet-based club where you can post your stories: www.cs.bilkent.edu.tr/~david/derya/ywc.html

Potluck Children's Literary Magazine at http://members.aol.com/potluckmagazine

Also check out: www.kidauthors.com for 6 to 18-year-olds.

Works quoted or mentioned in the text

Hacker, Malorie Blackman, Corgi

Five on a Treasure Island, Enid Blyton, Hodder Children's Books

Lionboy, Zizou Corder, Puffin

Wolf, Gillian Cross, Puffin

The Adventure of the Blue Carbuncle; The Adventure of the Speckled Band in *Sherlock Holmes Investigates*, Sir Arthur Conan Doyle

The Great Brain is Back. John D Fitzgerald, Dial Books

The Empty Sleeve, Leon Garfield, Viking Kestrel

SilverFin, Young Bond series, Charlie Higson, Puffin

Stormbreaker, Alex Rider series, Anthony Horowitz, Walker Books

Make No Mistake: Nancy Drew, Carolyn Keene, Pocket Books

A Place to Belong (The Orphan Train Adventures), Joan Lowery Nixon, Laurel Leaf

The Kidnapping of Christina Lattimore, Joan Lowery Nixon, Harcourt

Big Mouth and Ugly Girl, Joyce Carol Oates, Collins Flamingo

Dovey Coe, Frances O'Roark Dowell, Walker Books

The Ghost Belonged to Me, Richard Peck, Puffin

The Fall of the House of Usher in *Tales of Mystery and Imagination*, Edgar Allan Poe, Thomas Nelson

The Ruby in the Smoke, Philip Pullman, Scholastic